50 Ranch Sauce Dishes

By: Kelly Johnson

Table of Contents

- Classic Ranch Chicken Wings
- Ranch Chicken Salad
- Ranch Potato Salad
- Ranch Dip for Vegetables
- Ranch-Style Mac and Cheese
- Ranch Chicken Tenders
- Ranch Fries
- Ranch Grilled Vegetables
- Ranch Buffalo Cauliflower
- Ranch Pizza
- Ranch Dressing for Tacos
- Ranch Burger
- Ranch Slaw
- Ranch Bacon-Wrapped Shrimp
- Ranch Queso Dip
- Ranch Meatballs
- Ranch Wrap with Chicken
- Ranch-Crisped Potatoes
- Ranch Cauliflower Bites
- Ranch Roasted Chicken
- Ranch Cucumber Salad
- Ranch Pigs in a Blanket
- Ranch Deviled Eggs
- Ranch Roasted Brussels Sprouts
- Ranch Dip for Chips
- Ranch Pasta Salad
- Ranch Chicken Skewers
- Ranch Grilled Cheese
- Ranch Cheddar Biscuits
- Ranch Pork Chops
- Ranch-Stuffed Mushrooms
- Ranch Chicken Enchiladas
- Ranch Roasted Sweet Potatoes
- Ranch Spinach Artichoke Dip
- Ranch Cheddar Crackers

- Ranch Jalapeño Poppers
- Ranch Chicken and Rice Casserole
- Ranch Frittata
- Ranch Baked Ziti
- Ranch Tofu Tacos
- Ranch BBQ Chicken Pizza
- Ranch Avocado Toast
- Ranch Crab Cakes
- Ranch Buffalo Chicken Dip
- Ranch Grilled Salmon
- Ranch Caesar Salad
- Ranch-Glazed Pork Tenderloin
- Ranch Stuffed Peppers
- Ranch Veggie Skewers
- Ranch Spinach Salad

Classic Ranch Chicken Wings

Ingredients:

- 10 chicken wings
- 1/4 cup ranch dressing mix
- 2 tablespoons olive oil
- 1 tablespoon garlic powder
- 1 tablespoon onion powder
- Salt and pepper to taste
- 1/4 cup ranch dressing for dipping

Instructions:

1. Preheat the oven to 400°F (200°C).
2. In a bowl, toss the chicken wings with olive oil, ranch dressing mix, garlic powder, onion powder, salt, and pepper.
3. Arrange the wings on a baking sheet in a single layer.
4. Bake for 25-30 minutes, flipping halfway through, until golden and crispy.
5. Serve with ranch dressing for dipping.

Ranch Chicken Salad

Ingredients:

- 2 cups cooked chicken, shredded
- 1/2 cup ranch dressing
- 1/4 cup celery, chopped
- 1/4 cup red onion, diced
- 1/4 cup pickles, chopped
- Salt and pepper to taste
- Lettuce leaves for serving (optional)

Instructions:

1. In a large bowl, combine the shredded chicken, ranch dressing, celery, red onion, and pickles.
2. Season with salt and pepper.
3. Serve the chicken salad on a bed of lettuce or in a sandwich.

Ranch Potato Salad

Ingredients:

- 4 large potatoes, peeled and diced
- 1 cup ranch dressing
- 1/4 cup mayonnaise
- 1/4 cup red onion, finely chopped
- 2 hard-boiled eggs, chopped
- 1/4 cup fresh parsley, chopped
- Salt and pepper to taste

Instructions:

1. Boil the diced potatoes in salted water until tender, about 10-12 minutes. Drain and cool.
2. In a large bowl, mix the ranch dressing, mayonnaise, red onion, chopped eggs, and parsley.
3. Add the cooled potatoes to the dressing mixture and toss gently to combine.
4. Season with salt and pepper and refrigerate for 1 hour before serving.

Ranch Dip for Vegetables

Ingredients:

- 1 cup sour cream
- 1/2 cup mayonnaise
- 1 tablespoon ranch seasoning mix
- 1 tablespoon fresh dill, chopped (optional)
- Fresh vegetables like carrots, cucumbers, and bell peppers, cut into sticks

Instructions:

1. In a bowl, combine the sour cream, mayonnaise, ranch seasoning mix, and fresh dill.
2. Stir until smooth.
3. Serve with an assortment of fresh vegetables for dipping.

Ranch-Style Mac and Cheese

Ingredients:

- 1 lb elbow macaroni
- 2 cups shredded cheddar cheese
- 1 cup milk
- 1/4 cup butter
- 2 tablespoons all-purpose flour
- 1 packet ranch dressing mix
- Salt and pepper to taste

Instructions:

1. Cook the macaroni according to package instructions and drain.
2. In a saucepan, melt the butter over medium heat and whisk in the flour until smooth.
3. Gradually add the milk, whisking constantly until the sauce thickens.
4. Stir in the ranch seasoning mix and shredded cheddar cheese, and continue stirring until the cheese melts.
5. Toss the cooked macaroni in the sauce and season with salt and pepper.

Ranch Chicken Tenders

Ingredients:

- 1 lb chicken tenders
- 1/2 cup ranch dressing
- 1/2 cup breadcrumbs
- 1/4 cup grated Parmesan cheese
- 1 tablespoon garlic powder
- Salt and pepper to taste

Instructions:

1. Preheat the oven to 375°F (190°C).
2. Dip each chicken tender in ranch dressing, then coat with a mixture of breadcrumbs, Parmesan cheese, garlic powder, salt, and pepper.
3. Place the chicken tenders on a baking sheet and bake for 20-25 minutes, until golden and cooked through.
4. Serve with extra ranch dressing for dipping.

Ranch Fries

Ingredients:

- 4 large potatoes, cut into wedges
- 2 tablespoons olive oil
- 1 tablespoon ranch seasoning mix
- Salt and pepper to taste

Instructions:

1. Preheat the oven to 425°F (220°C).
2. Toss the potato wedges in olive oil and ranch seasoning mix until evenly coated.
3. Arrange the wedges on a baking sheet in a single layer.
4. Bake for 25-30 minutes, flipping halfway through, until crispy and golden.
5. Serve with ranch dressing or ketchup.

Ranch Grilled Vegetables

Ingredients:

- 2 cups mixed vegetables (such as bell peppers, zucchini, and mushrooms)
- 2 tablespoons olive oil
- 1 tablespoon ranch seasoning mix
- Salt and pepper to taste

Instructions:

1. Preheat the grill to medium-high heat.
2. Toss the vegetables in olive oil and ranch seasoning.
3. Grill the vegetables for 4-5 minutes per side until tender and lightly charred.
4. Serve warm as a side dish.

Ranch Buffalo Cauliflower

Ingredients:

- 1 head of cauliflower, cut into florets
- 1/4 cup ranch dressing
- 1/4 cup buffalo sauce
- 1 tablespoon olive oil
- 1 tablespoon garlic powder
- Salt and pepper to taste

Instructions:

1. Preheat the oven to 400°F (200°C).
2. Toss the cauliflower florets with olive oil, garlic powder, salt, and pepper.
3. Roast the cauliflower for 20-25 minutes, turning halfway through, until golden and tender.
4. In a separate bowl, mix the ranch dressing and buffalo sauce.
5. Toss the roasted cauliflower in the ranch-buffalo sauce mixture.
6. Serve immediately as a spicy, tangy appetizer or side.

Ranch Pizza

Ingredients:

- 1 pizza dough
- 1/2 cup ranch dressing (as the base sauce)
- 1 cup shredded mozzarella cheese
- 1/2 cup cooked chicken, shredded
- 1/4 cup red onion, thinly sliced
- 1/4 cup green bell pepper, thinly sliced
- 1/4 cup cooked bacon bits
- Fresh parsley, chopped (for garnish)

Instructions:

1. Preheat the oven to 475°F (245°C).
2. Roll out the pizza dough on a floured surface to your desired thickness.
3. Spread the ranch dressing evenly over the dough, leaving a small border around the edges.
4. Sprinkle the shredded mozzarella cheese over the ranch dressing.
5. Top with shredded chicken, red onion, green bell pepper, and bacon bits.
6. Bake in the oven for 10-12 minutes, until the crust is golden and the cheese is bubbly.
7. Remove from the oven and garnish with fresh parsley. Slice and serve!

Ranch Dressing for Tacos

Ingredients:

- 1/2 cup ranch dressing
- 1 tablespoon lime juice
- 1 tablespoon chopped cilantro
- 1/2 teaspoon garlic powder
- 1/2 teaspoon cumin
- Salt and pepper to taste

Instructions:

1. In a small bowl, mix together the ranch dressing, lime juice, cilantro, garlic powder, cumin, salt, and pepper.
2. Stir until well combined.
3. Drizzle the ranch dressing over your tacos for a creamy, tangy twist!

Ranch Burger

Ingredients:

- 1 lb ground beef (or chicken/turkey)
- 1 packet ranch seasoning mix
- 4 burger buns
- 1/2 cup ranch dressing
- Lettuce, tomato, and onion for toppings

Instructions:

1. Preheat a grill or skillet over medium heat.
2. Mix the ground beef with the ranch seasoning mix and form into 4 patties.
3. Cook the patties for 4-5 minutes per side or until fully cooked.
4. Toast the burger buns on the grill or in a skillet until lightly browned.
5. Spread ranch dressing on the bottom bun, then place the cooked patty on top.
6. Add your favorite toppings like lettuce, tomato, and onion, and serve!

Ranch Slaw

Ingredients:

- 4 cups shredded cabbage
- 1/2 cup ranch dressing
- 1/4 cup mayonnaise
- 1 tablespoon apple cider vinegar
- 1 tablespoon sugar
- 1/4 teaspoon celery seed
- Salt and pepper to taste

Instructions:

1. In a large bowl, combine the shredded cabbage, ranch dressing, mayonnaise, vinegar, sugar, and celery seed.
2. Toss the mixture until the cabbage is evenly coated.
3. Season with salt and pepper, then refrigerate for at least 30 minutes before serving.

Ranch Bacon-Wrapped Shrimp

Ingredients:

- 12 large shrimp, peeled and deveined
- 12 slices bacon
- 1/4 cup ranch dressing
- 1 tablespoon fresh parsley, chopped (for garnish)

Instructions:

1. Preheat the oven to 400°F (200°C).
2. Wrap each shrimp with a slice of bacon, securing with toothpicks.
3. Place the bacon-wrapped shrimp on a baking sheet.
4. Bake for 12-15 minutes, or until the bacon is crispy and the shrimp are cooked through.
5. Drizzle with ranch dressing and garnish with fresh parsley before serving.

Ranch Queso Dip

Ingredients:

- 1 cup ranch dressing
- 8 oz cream cheese, softened
- 1 cup shredded cheddar cheese
- 1/4 cup diced green chilies
- 1 tablespoon taco seasoning

Instructions:

1. In a medium saucepan, combine the ranch dressing and cream cheese. Heat over medium heat, stirring until smooth.
2. Add the shredded cheddar cheese, diced green chilies, and taco seasoning. Stir until the cheese is melted and the dip is creamy.
3. Serve warm with tortilla chips or fresh veggies for dipping.

Ranch Meatballs

Ingredients:

- 1 lb ground beef (or turkey)
- 1 packet ranch seasoning mix
- 1/4 cup breadcrumbs
- 1 egg
- 1/4 cup grated Parmesan cheese

Instructions:

1. Preheat the oven to 375°F (190°C).
2. In a large bowl, mix the ground beef, ranch seasoning, breadcrumbs, egg, and Parmesan cheese.
3. Form the mixture into small meatballs and place them on a baking sheet.
4. Bake for 15-20 minutes, or until the meatballs are cooked through.
5. Serve with ranch dressing for dipping.

Ranch Wrap with Chicken

Ingredients:

- 2 cups cooked chicken, shredded
- 2 large tortillas
- 1/4 cup ranch dressing
- 1 cup lettuce, shredded
- 1/2 cup shredded cheese
- 1/4 cup diced tomatoes
- 1/4 cup red onion, sliced

Instructions:

1. Spread ranch dressing evenly over each tortilla.
2. Layer with shredded chicken, lettuce, shredded cheese, diced tomatoes, and red onion.
3. Roll up the tortillas tightly and slice them into wraps.
4. Serve with extra ranch dressing for dipping.

Ranch-Crisped Potatoes

Ingredients:

- 4 medium potatoes, cut into wedges
- 1 tablespoon ranch seasoning mix
- 2 tablespoons olive oil
- Salt and pepper to taste

Instructions:

1. Preheat the oven to 425°F (220°C).
2. Toss the potato wedges with olive oil, ranch seasoning mix, salt, and pepper.
3. Arrange the potatoes on a baking sheet in a single layer.
4. Bake for 30-35 minutes, flipping halfway through, until the potatoes are golden and crispy.
5. Serve as a side dish or snack with ranch dressing for dipping.

Ranch Cauliflower Bites

Ingredients:

- 1 medium cauliflower, cut into florets
- 1/2 cup ranch dressing
- 1/4 cup grated Parmesan cheese
- 1 tablespoon olive oil
- Salt and pepper to taste
- Fresh parsley (for garnish)

Instructions:

1. Preheat the oven to 400°F (200°C).
2. In a large bowl, toss the cauliflower florets with olive oil, ranch dressing, Parmesan cheese, salt, and pepper.
3. Spread the cauliflower out in a single layer on a baking sheet.
4. Roast for 20-25 minutes, flipping halfway through, until the cauliflower is golden and tender.
5. Garnish with fresh parsley and serve as a delicious snack or side dish.

Ranch Roasted Chicken

Ingredients:

- 1 whole chicken (about 4 lbs)
- 1/4 cup ranch seasoning mix
- 2 tablespoons olive oil
- Salt and pepper to taste
- Fresh herbs (like rosemary or thyme, for garnish)

Instructions:

1. Preheat the oven to 425°F (220°C).
2. Rub the chicken with olive oil, ranch seasoning mix, salt, and pepper.
3. Place the chicken on a roasting pan and roast for 1-1.5 hours, or until the internal temperature reaches 165°F (75°C).
4. Let the chicken rest for 10 minutes before carving. Garnish with fresh herbs and serve with your favorite sides.

Ranch Cucumber Salad

Ingredients:

- 2 cups cucumber, thinly sliced
- 1/4 cup ranch dressing
- 1 tablespoon white vinegar
- 1 tablespoon fresh dill, chopped
- 1/4 red onion, thinly sliced
- Salt and pepper to taste

Instructions:

1. In a large bowl, combine the cucumber, red onion, and fresh dill.
2. Drizzle with ranch dressing and white vinegar.
3. Toss until well coated, then season with salt and pepper.
4. Chill for 15-20 minutes before serving to let the flavors meld.

Ranch Pigs in a Blanket

Ingredients:

- 1 package mini cocktail sausages
- 1 can crescent roll dough
- 1/4 cup ranch dressing
- 1 tablespoon chopped chives

Instructions:

1. Preheat the oven according to the crescent roll dough package instructions.
2. Unroll the dough and cut it into small strips that will wrap around the sausages.
3. Wrap each sausage in dough and place them on a baking sheet.
4. Bake according to the package instructions until golden and crispy.
5. Drizzle with ranch dressing and sprinkle with chives before serving.

Ranch Deviled Eggs

Ingredients:

- 6 hard-boiled eggs, peeled and halved
- 1/4 cup ranch dressing
- 1 tablespoon mayonnaise
- 1 teaspoon mustard
- 1/4 teaspoon garlic powder
- Salt and pepper to taste
- Paprika (for garnish)

Instructions:

1. Scoop the yolks out of the boiled egg halves and place them in a bowl.
2. Mash the yolks and mix with ranch dressing, mayonnaise, mustard, garlic powder, salt, and pepper until smooth.
3. Spoon or pipe the mixture back into the egg whites.
4. Sprinkle with paprika and serve chilled.

Ranch Roasted Brussels Sprouts

Ingredients:

- 1 lb Brussels sprouts, trimmed and halved
- 1/4 cup ranch dressing
- 2 tablespoons olive oil
- Salt and pepper to taste

Instructions:

1. Preheat the oven to 400°F (200°C).
2. In a large bowl, toss the Brussels sprouts with olive oil, ranch dressing, salt, and pepper.
3. Spread them on a baking sheet in a single layer.
4. Roast for 20-25 minutes, shaking the pan halfway through, until golden brown and crispy on the edges.
5. Serve as a savory side dish.

Ranch Dip for Chips

Ingredients:

- 1 cup ranch dressing
- 1/2 cup sour cream
- 1 tablespoon lemon juice
- 1/2 teaspoon garlic powder
- Salt and pepper to taste

Instructions:

1. In a bowl, combine ranch dressing, sour cream, lemon juice, garlic powder, salt, and pepper.
2. Stir until smooth and well combined.
3. Serve with your favorite chips for dipping.

Ranch Pasta Salad

Ingredients:

- 3 cups cooked pasta (any shape)
- 1/2 cup ranch dressing
- 1/4 cup mayonnaise
- 1/4 cup diced cucumber
- 1/4 cup diced red bell pepper
- 1/4 cup sliced black olives
- Salt and pepper to taste

Instructions:

1. In a large bowl, combine the cooked pasta, ranch dressing, and mayonnaise.
2. Add in the diced cucumber, red bell pepper, and sliced black olives.
3. Toss until the pasta and veggies are well coated.
4. Season with salt and pepper, then chill in the fridge for at least 30 minutes before serving.

Ranch Chicken Skewers

Ingredients:

- 2 lbs chicken breast, cut into cubes
- 1/4 cup ranch dressing
- 1 tablespoon olive oil
- 1 teaspoon garlic powder
- 1 teaspoon paprika
- Salt and pepper to taste
- Skewers (wooden or metal)

Instructions:

1. Preheat the grill to medium-high heat.
2. In a bowl, mix ranch dressing, olive oil, garlic powder, paprika, salt, and pepper.
3. Thread the chicken cubes onto the skewers.
4. Brush the ranch mixture over the chicken.
5. Grill for 6-8 minutes on each side or until the chicken is cooked through.
6. Serve with extra ranch dressing for dipping.

Ranch Grilled Cheese

Ingredients:

- 2 slices of bread
- 2 tablespoons ranch dressing
- 1/2 cup shredded cheddar cheese
- 1 tablespoon butter

Instructions:

1. Preheat a skillet over medium heat.
2. Spread ranch dressing on one side of each slice of bread.
3. Add shredded cheddar cheese between the slices of bread, with the ranch dressing sides facing out.
4. Butter the outside of the bread slices.
5. Grill in the skillet for 2-3 minutes per side or until golden brown and the cheese has melted.
6. Serve hot and enjoy!

Ranch Cheddar Biscuits

Ingredients:

- 2 cups all-purpose flour
- 2 teaspoons baking powder
- 1/2 teaspoon salt
- 1/2 cup cold butter, cubed
- 1 cup shredded cheddar cheese
- 1/2 cup buttermilk
- 1/4 cup ranch dressing

Instructions:

1. Preheat the oven to 425°F (220°C).
2. In a bowl, combine the flour, baking powder, and salt.
3. Cut the cold butter into the dry ingredients until it resembles coarse crumbs.
4. Add shredded cheddar cheese and mix.
5. In a separate bowl, whisk together the buttermilk and ranch dressing.
6. Pour the wet ingredients into the dry ingredients and stir until just combined.
7. Drop spoonfuls of the dough onto a baking sheet.
8. Bake for 12-15 minutes until golden brown.
9. Serve warm with extra ranch dressing if desired.

Ranch Pork Chops

Ingredients:

- 4 bone-in pork chops
- 1/4 cup ranch dressing
- 2 tablespoons olive oil
- 1 teaspoon garlic powder
- 1 teaspoon dried thyme
- Salt and pepper to taste

Instructions:

1. Preheat the oven to 375°F (190°C).
2. Rub the pork chops with olive oil, ranch dressing, garlic powder, thyme, salt, and pepper.
3. Place the pork chops on a baking sheet and bake for 25-30 minutes, or until the internal temperature reaches 145°F (63°C).
4. Let the pork chops rest for 5 minutes before serving.

Ranch-Stuffed Mushrooms

Ingredients:

- 12 large mushroom caps
- 1/2 cup ranch dressing
- 1/4 cup grated Parmesan cheese
- 1/2 cup breadcrumbs
- 1 tablespoon olive oil
- 2 tablespoons chopped parsley
- Salt and pepper to taste

Instructions:

1. Preheat the oven to 375°F (190°C).
2. Remove the stems from the mushrooms and place the caps on a baking sheet.
3. In a bowl, combine ranch dressing, Parmesan cheese, breadcrumbs, olive oil, parsley, salt, and pepper.
4. Spoon the mixture into the mushroom caps.
5. Bake for 15-20 minutes until the mushrooms are tender and the stuffing is golden brown.
6. Serve hot as an appetizer or side dish.

Ranch Chicken Enchiladas

Ingredients:

- 2 cups cooked, shredded chicken
- 1/2 cup ranch dressing
- 1 can enchilada sauce
- 8 flour tortillas
- 2 cups shredded cheddar cheese
- 1/2 cup chopped green onions

Instructions:

1. Preheat the oven to 350°F (175°C).
2. In a bowl, mix the shredded chicken with ranch dressing and 1/4 cup of the enchilada sauce.
3. Warm the tortillas in the microwave for 20-30 seconds to make them more pliable.
4. Spread a small amount of enchilada sauce on the bottom of a baking dish.
5. Fill each tortilla with the chicken mixture, roll up, and place seam-side down in the baking dish.
6. Pour the remaining enchilada sauce over the top of the rolled tortillas and sprinkle with shredded cheese.
7. Bake for 20-25 minutes until the cheese is melted and bubbly.
8. Garnish with chopped green onions before serving.

Ranch Roasted Sweet Potatoes

Ingredients:

- 2 large sweet potatoes, peeled and cubed
- 2 tablespoons olive oil
- 1/4 cup ranch dressing
- 1 teaspoon paprika
- Salt and pepper to taste

Instructions:

1. Preheat the oven to 400°F (200°C).
2. Toss the cubed sweet potatoes with olive oil, ranch dressing, paprika, salt, and pepper.
3. Spread the potatoes in a single layer on a baking sheet.
4. Roast for 25-30 minutes, stirring halfway through, until the potatoes are golden brown and tender.
5. Serve as a side dish.

Ranch Spinach Artichoke Dip

Ingredients:

- 1 cup ranch dressing
- 1 can (14 oz) artichoke hearts, drained and chopped
- 1 cup cooked spinach, squeezed dry
- 1 cup cream cheese, softened
- 1/2 cup grated Parmesan cheese
- 1/2 cup shredded mozzarella cheese

Instructions:

1. Preheat the oven to 375°F (190°C).
2. In a mixing bowl, combine ranch dressing, artichoke hearts, spinach, cream cheese, Parmesan, and mozzarella cheese.
3. Transfer the mixture to a baking dish and bake for 20-25 minutes, until the top is golden and bubbly.
4. Serve with crackers, tortilla chips, or vegetable sticks.

Ranch Cheddar Crackers

Ingredients:

- 1 1/2 cups all-purpose flour
- 1/2 cup shredded cheddar cheese
- 2 tablespoons ranch seasoning mix
- 1/4 cup cold butter, cubed
- 2-3 tablespoons cold water

Instructions:

1. Preheat the oven to 350°F (175°C).
2. In a food processor, combine the flour, cheddar cheese, and ranch seasoning.
3. Add cold butter and pulse until the mixture resembles coarse crumbs.
4. Add cold water, 1 tablespoon at a time, until the dough comes together.
5. Roll out the dough on a floured surface to 1/8 inch thick and cut into small squares.
6. Place on a baking sheet and bake for 12-15 minutes, or until golden and crisp.
7. Cool and serve as a crunchy snack.

Ranch Jalapeño Poppers

Ingredients:

- 12 large jalapeños, halved and seeded
- 8 oz cream cheese, softened
- 1/4 cup ranch dressing
- 1 cup shredded cheddar cheese
- 1/2 cup cooked and crumbled bacon
- 1 tablespoon chopped green onions
- 1/2 cup breadcrumbs

Instructions:

1. Preheat the oven to 375°F (190°C).
2. Mix cream cheese, ranch dressing, cheddar cheese, crumbled bacon, and green onions in a bowl.
3. Stuff each jalapeño half with the cream cheese mixture.
4. Dip the stuffed jalapeños in breadcrumbs, then place them on a baking sheet.
5. Bake for 15-20 minutes, or until the breadcrumbs are golden and the jalapeños are tender.
6. Serve hot as an appetizer.

Ranch Chicken and Rice Casserole

Ingredients:

- 2 cups cooked chicken, shredded
- 1 cup rice, uncooked
- 1/4 cup ranch dressing
- 1 can cream of chicken soup
- 1 cup chicken broth
- 1 cup shredded cheddar cheese
- Salt and pepper to taste

Instructions:

1. Preheat the oven to 350°F (175°C).
2. In a bowl, combine ranch dressing, cream of chicken soup, chicken broth, and cooked chicken.
3. Add uncooked rice, salt, and pepper, and mix everything together.
4. Transfer the mixture to a greased 9x13 baking dish.
5. Cover with foil and bake for 30-35 minutes, then uncover and bake for an additional 10-15 minutes until the rice is cooked and the casserole is bubbly.
6. Sprinkle with shredded cheddar cheese and bake for 5 more minutes until the cheese is melted.
7. Serve and enjoy!

Ranch Frittata

Ingredients:

- 6 large eggs
- 1/4 cup ranch dressing
- 1/2 cup shredded cheddar cheese
- 1/4 cup diced bell peppers
- 1/4 cup chopped spinach
- 1/4 cup diced onions
- Salt and pepper to taste

Instructions:

1. Preheat the oven to 375°F (190°C).
2. In a bowl, whisk together eggs, ranch dressing, salt, and pepper.
3. Stir in shredded cheese, bell peppers, spinach, and onions.
4. Pour the egg mixture into a greased oven-safe skillet.
5. Bake for 20-25 minutes, until the eggs are set and the top is golden brown.
6. Serve warm for breakfast or brunch.

Ranch Baked Ziti

Ingredients:

- 1 pound ziti pasta
- 1 jar marinara sauce
- 1/2 cup ranch dressing
- 1/2 cup ricotta cheese
- 2 cups shredded mozzarella cheese
- 1/2 cup grated Parmesan cheese

Instructions:

1. Preheat the oven to 350°F (175°C).
2. Cook the ziti pasta according to the package directions, drain, and set aside.
3. In a bowl, mix marinara sauce, ranch dressing, and ricotta cheese.
4. Combine the cooked pasta with the sauce mixture.
5. Transfer to a baking dish, then top with shredded mozzarella and Parmesan cheeses.
6. Bake for 20-25 minutes, until the cheese is melted and bubbly.
7. Serve hot and enjoy!

Ranch Tofu Tacos

Ingredients:

- 1 block firm tofu, drained and crumbled
- 1/4 cup ranch dressing
- 1 teaspoon garlic powder
- 1 teaspoon cumin
- 1 teaspoon paprika
- Salt and pepper to taste
- Soft corn or flour tortillas
- Toppings: shredded lettuce, diced tomatoes, avocado, salsa, cilantro

Instructions:

1. In a skillet over medium heat, cook crumbled tofu with ranch dressing, garlic powder, cumin, paprika, salt, and pepper for 5-7 minutes until heated through and slightly crispy.
2. Warm the tortillas and fill them with the seasoned tofu mixture.
3. Top with lettuce, tomatoes, avocado, salsa, and cilantro.
4. Serve immediately for a delicious vegetarian taco option.

Ranch BBQ Chicken Pizza

Ingredients:

- 1 pizza crust (store-bought or homemade)
- 1 cup cooked, shredded chicken
- 1/4 cup ranch dressing
- 1/4 cup BBQ sauce
- 1 cup shredded mozzarella cheese
- 1/2 red onion, thinly sliced
- 1/2 cup corn kernels (optional)
- 1/4 cup chopped cilantro

Instructions:

1. Preheat the oven according to the pizza crust instructions.
2. Mix the cooked chicken with ranch dressing and BBQ sauce.
3. Spread the chicken mixture evenly over the pizza crust.
4. Top with shredded mozzarella cheese, red onion slices, and corn (if using).
5. Bake the pizza according to the crust instructions, usually 12-15 minutes, until the crust is golden and the cheese is melted.
6. Garnish with chopped cilantro before serving.

Ranch Avocado Toast

Ingredients:

- 2 slices of bread (your choice)
- 1 ripe avocado
- 2 tablespoons ranch dressing
- Salt and pepper to taste
- Optional toppings: cherry tomatoes, red onion, microgreens

Instructions:

1. Toast the bread to your desired crispiness.
2. Mash the avocado in a bowl and mix in ranch dressing, salt, and pepper.
3. Spread the avocado mixture onto the toasted bread.
4. Top with any optional toppings like cherry tomatoes or microgreens.
5. Serve immediately for a creamy, flavorful breakfast or snack.

Ranch Crab Cakes

Ingredients:

- 1 lb lump crab meat
- 1/2 cup breadcrumbs
- 1/4 cup ranch dressing
- 1 tablespoon Dijon mustard
- 1 egg
- 1 tablespoon chopped parsley
- Salt and pepper to taste
- Olive oil for frying

Instructions:

1. In a bowl, mix together crab meat, breadcrumbs, ranch dressing, Dijon mustard, egg, parsley, salt, and pepper.
2. Form the mixture into small patties.
3. Heat olive oil in a skillet over medium heat.
4. Fry the crab cakes for 3-4 minutes on each side until golden brown and crispy.
5. Serve with a side of ranch dressing or your favorite dipping sauce.

Ranch Buffalo Chicken Dip

Ingredients:

- 2 cups cooked shredded chicken
- 1/2 cup ranch dressing
- 1/2 cup buffalo sauce
- 8 oz cream cheese, softened
- 1 cup shredded cheddar cheese
- 1/2 cup blue cheese crumbles (optional)

Instructions:

1. Preheat the oven to 350°F (175°C).
2. In a bowl, combine shredded chicken, ranch dressing, buffalo sauce, cream cheese, and shredded cheddar cheese.
3. Transfer the mixture to a baking dish and spread evenly.
4. Top with blue cheese crumbles (if using) and bake for 20 minutes, until bubbly and hot.
5. Serve with tortilla chips, celery sticks, or crackers for dipping.

Ranch Grilled Salmon

Ingredients:

- 4 salmon fillets
- 1/4 cup ranch dressing
- 1 tablespoon olive oil
- 1 tablespoon lemon juice
- 1 teaspoon garlic powder
- Salt and pepper to taste
- Fresh parsley for garnish

Instructions:

1. Preheat the grill to medium heat.
2. In a small bowl, mix ranch dressing, olive oil, lemon juice, garlic powder, salt, and pepper.
3. Brush the salmon fillets with the ranch dressing mixture on both sides.
4. Grill the salmon for about 4-5 minutes per side, until cooked through and slightly crispy on the edges.
5. Garnish with fresh parsley and serve with a side of your choice.

Ranch Caesar Salad

Ingredients:

- 4 cups romaine lettuce, chopped
- 1/4 cup ranch dressing
- 1/4 cup Caesar dressing
- 1/2 cup croutons
- 1/4 cup grated Parmesan cheese

Instructions:

1. In a large bowl, combine the romaine lettuce with ranch dressing and Caesar dressing. Toss until evenly coated.
2. Add croutons and grated Parmesan cheese, then toss again.
3. Serve immediately for a creamy and tangy twist on the classic Caesar salad.

Ranch-Glazed Pork Tenderloin

Ingredients:

- 1 pork tenderloin (about 1 lb)
- 1/4 cup ranch dressing
- 2 tablespoons honey
- 1 tablespoon Dijon mustard
- 1 teaspoon garlic powder
- Salt and pepper to taste

Instructions:

1. Preheat the oven to 400°F (200°C).
2. In a small bowl, mix ranch dressing, honey, Dijon mustard, garlic powder, salt, and pepper.
3. Rub the pork tenderloin with the ranch glaze, coating it evenly.
4. Place the tenderloin on a baking sheet and bake for 25-30 minutes, or until the pork reaches an internal temperature of 145°F (63°C).
5. Let the pork rest for 5 minutes before slicing and serving.

Ranch Stuffed Peppers

Ingredients:

- 4 large bell peppers, tops cut off and seeds removed
- 1 lb ground beef or turkey
- 1/2 cup cooked rice
- 1/4 cup ranch dressing
- 1/2 cup shredded cheddar cheese
- 1 teaspoon garlic powder
- Salt and pepper to taste

Instructions:

1. Preheat the oven to 375°F (190°C).
2. In a skillet, cook the ground meat with garlic powder, salt, and pepper until browned.
3. In a bowl, mix the cooked meat, rice, ranch dressing, and half of the shredded cheese.
4. Stuff the peppers with the mixture and place them in a baking dish.
5. Top with the remaining shredded cheese and bake for 25-30 minutes, until the peppers are tender and the cheese is melted.
6. Serve hot and enjoy!

Ranch Veggie Skewers

Ingredients:

- 1 zucchini, sliced
- 1 bell pepper, cut into chunks
- 1 red onion, cut into chunks
- 1 cup cherry tomatoes
- 1/4 cup ranch dressing
- Salt and pepper to taste
- Olive oil for grilling

Instructions:

1. Preheat the grill to medium heat.
2. Thread the zucchini, bell pepper, onion, and cherry tomatoes onto skewers.
3. Brush the vegetables with ranch dressing and season with salt and pepper.
4. Grill the skewers for about 10 minutes, turning occasionally, until the vegetables are tender and lightly charred.
5. Serve as a side dish or light main course.

Ranch Spinach Salad

Ingredients:

- 4 cups fresh spinach leaves
- 1/2 cup ranch dressing
- 1/4 cup sliced red onion
- 1/2 cup sliced strawberries
- 1/4 cup sunflower seeds
- 1/4 cup feta cheese, crumbled

Instructions:

1. In a large bowl, combine the spinach, red onion, strawberries, sunflower seeds, and feta cheese.
2. Drizzle with ranch dressing and toss gently to coat.
3. Serve immediately as a fresh and tangy salad perfect for any meal.

www.ingramcontent.com/pod-product-compliance
Lightning Source LLC
LaVergne TN
LVHW081502060526
838201LV00056BA/2883